Time Winds

poems by

Alfred Kisubi

BkMk Press
University of Missouri-Kansas City

An International / Translation Series Book

ACKNOWLEDGMENTS

Poems in this book have appeared in *The Sunbirds* (Makerere University, Uganda), *Kenya Times* (Nairobi), *Minds Eye* (Johnson County Community College, Kansas), *Men Only* (Nairobi), *Anthology of Azania Poems* (Boston), *International Student Newsletter* (Kansas City), The Sametan (Kenya), *Kiira College Magazine* (Uganda).

Time Winds was originally published with the help and under the joint aegis of the Johnson County Community College (Johnson County, Kansas) and its International Educational Program. Alfred Kisubi first came to the United States under the auspices of that program.

Thanks to Carolyn Kadel, Coordinator of International Education; Landon Kirchner, Director of Division of Humanities and Social Sciences; and Robert Burdick, Director of College Information and Publications, all of J.C.C.C., whose support made this volume possible. Also to Prof. David Binkley of the U.M.K.C. Dept. of Art and a curator of the Nelson-Atkins Museum of Art and to Doren Ross, Associate Director, Museum of Cultural History at U.C.L.A. for their help in providing authentic African artwork for the jacket and book. Appreciation is due the Museum of Cultural History (photos by Richard Todd) for permission to reprint material from Igbo Art Community & Cosmos.

Library of Congress Cataloging Publication Data
Kisubi, Alfred
Time Winds
(An International/translation series book)
1. Uganda—Poetry. I. Title II. Series
PR9402.9.K57T56 1986   821   87-72130
ISBN: 0-933532-95-4

BkMk Press
University of Missouri-Kansas City
5101 Rockhill Road
Kansas City, Missouri, 64110-2499

DEDICATION

With hope for Uganda,
To my mother and in memory of my father,
With love for Carrie Gallagher
And Bob Perry,
Chuck Bishop and Carolyn Kadel,
Richard and Rhene Tantala,
Dr. Linda Breytspraak and Dr. Oscar Eggers,
Then Susan Gray, Victoria Spain,
And all in Kenya, Tanzania,
And people of the USA who lent me their hearts
For no price.

.

CONTENTS

Introduction   7

These Pigs   9
At the Celebration of Freedom   10
Kilembe Mines   11
Termites   12
25TH of January   13
Clara of Lorina Club   14
Here We Are   15
Predators   16
Suddenly   16
The Freedom Embrace   17
The Teak Tree at Mabira   18
Old Pain   19

I Speared and Spilled   20
A Girl's Love Song   21
A Jilt   22
The Love Pistol   23
The Wedding   24
A Good Husband Rarely Smokes at Home   25
Njeri of Nyeri   26
Barren Woman   27
No More   28

Twelve Hours   29
The Handicapped Hand-Cuffed   30
From the Office Chair   31
Pointing Fingers   32
Teeth   33
Rats in the Lodge   34
Malaria   35
City Kid   36
VIP at the Slums ?   37

Before and After   38
I Will Grow   39
The Lady at Kisenyi   40
The Wind and the Storm   41
Sons of Wanga   42
Various Frames   43
Getting Stuck   44
Echoes to a Liberator at War   45
Drowned in the Murmuring Crowd   46
Labour Ward   47
Too Young   48
Losing the War in Azania-Namibia   49
Rascals   50
Third World War   51
Condominium Pandemonium   52
Summit on World Poverty   53
The Global Juke Box — July 13, 1985   54

August First   55
Essay on Poetry   56
The Eagles   57
Orchids   58
Migrating Storks   59
To My Jogging Mate   60

A Call from Grandee   62
Childhood Memories   65
The Black Pot of Potatoes   66
Smithies in Kisenyi   67
Greetings   68
A Paean for P'Bitek   71

Glossary   74

Introduction

Alfred Kisubi is a poet who walked into Kenya out of the remnants of Idi Amin's Uganda. While in Kenya, as the result of a friendship with an American sociologist and Peace Corps volunteer, Robert L. Perry, Kisubi was invited to become a faculty member of Johnson County Community College in Overland Park, Kansas.

And so with scant baggage and many poems, he came to our awareness. Read his poems and you will become immediately conscious that his English, rhythmically and idiomatically lithe and powerful, is as distinct from ours as American English is from British English. That makes his poems a bit more difficult, but also more intriguing, unusual, and authentic.

Alfred Kisubi is among other things a sociologist, a veterinarian, a folk-artist, and a student of religion. Currently he is doing research in gerontology. But first he is a poet of unusual scope and dexterity. He has a budding reputation in Africa as a result of publications in the *Kenya Times*, but he is generally unknown elsewhere. We hope the publication of *Time Winds* will enhance his reputation.

These poems demonstrate what has always been true of major writers: great feeling, ample skill, and significant concerns. They also continuously reflect Kisubi's origins. They allude often to the Amin era, its terror and unpredictability. Says Kisubi, quoting a bit of ancient lore, "Living in the jungle one may consider elephants as friends, but one does not know when the lions will attack." These poems are full of echoes of Lusoga, Kisubi's mother tongue. Variant lines in these poems derive from the spoken rhythms of that African language: "At long last the pearly black pot," scanned is such a line. Readers of these poems will march to an African drummer. They will learn *K'la* means Kampala, the capital of Uganda. They will come to realize the enormous diversity of tribal customs, and they will also realize the richness and difficulty that have produced a poet of this stature.

Alfred Kisubi says his prodigious output he once drafted (600 poems in one year) results from trying to photograph situations he has been through. He sees poems as "files to keep experience in." In Uganda he saw death directly. As a consequence, his purpose is to show "images of pain, of people going through it," so that his larger theme may be realized: "Don't brutalize each other." He believes that "the world is for all of us." He believes in "an unconditional love for people," and in peaceful transitions in human development. Says Kisubi, "People who make war do not understand *they* can die in war." At the same time he believes the poet's purpose is to be more than a spokesman or a feeling observer. "Language," says Kisubi, "must be reconstructed by the poet."

Alfred Kisubi pays homage to Okot P'Bitek, his former professor and poet of Uganda. Bitek quarrelled with the status quo for its excessiveness and for what it overlooked. *Time Winds* includes an elegy to this great writer.

Kisubi says, "I believe that I must do with what I have." What he clearly has is an extraordinary talent to share.

—*Dan Jaffe*

These Pigs
(*For George Orwell*)

We are rabbits eating our droppings
To digest the meagre remaining legnin,
Ruminant cows chewing hard cud,
To churn the roughage of the day.

They,
The pigs, with simple stomachs
Chew softly and digest easily our flesh.
Using their sharp ears,
To detect the soft swill.

At the Celebration of Freedom

The phalanx slowly marches
Perfunctorily through Freedom Square;
Their long faces, a miserable desert landscape,
Their dilating eyes, bloodshot but sleepy,
Their hands, lean and limply lanky,
Their legs, mechanical drumsticks,
Their Cow-dung-green, bleached pale
By recent storms, sunshines
And skirmishes.
      Dirtied by dry dust,
Their revolver straps,
Like their hearts, broken,
Self-confidence once alight
And bright, extinguished!
Hopes, haste and helmets gone,
Only platoons of school children
Policed parade through empty streets
Slowly waving the victory flag
Through the silence broken by sad sounds
Of a long regimental band.

Kilembe Mines

In the dark, like this,
When the miner's friends go away,
They take away his heart.

When they return
On the wake of another day, like this,
He hides his heart
In the subterranean cells,
For he must not reveal his pettiness.

All the same, all day
There he is, working,
There he is, cracking
Jokes and stones
In the quarry of his life.

Termites

Heavily armed
They ransack: rucksacks, gunnysacks
goatskin bags, handbags, grubby headloads,
cases, crates, cartons, briefcases and bales

In cold dark tunnels
They condemn condescension, forcing confession
From conformists and heretics,
They retain radio cassettes and tapes
Suspected to be more subversive than the owners
Who're sometimes free to quickly go, without the machines!

In searching scrutiny,
They pat—pat and palpate pockets
On palpitating breast, they paw
For cigarettes prejudicial to state lungs,
But apparently safe for them to puff—
As they sip intoxicant soda, on duty!

In vigilant strictness,
They occasionally arrest a *magendoist*
Shake a friendly clenched hand with him
And let him go—
Only uncourteous unscrupulosity
Monsterous to the state and the citizen
Would commit an innocent to Court!

They all quickly look furtively round
Then shoot money into pockets,
So many strict security vigilantes
Can't be wrong, year after year
So they play on the song.

25th of January

I switched my TV set,
I did, but it was blurred,
Was there a storm in the city?

Suddenly, I saw him
Covering the whole screen,
There, I saw him,
An   on his right
Another on his left,
His magic wand in hand.
I switched off the set.

I switched on my radio
Only to hear a special announcement:
"Hence, I repeat hence...
You'll call me blessed
To be for life or king of kings
For he who is mighty
Like the Almighty
Has coined a new era for you and me."
I switched off the radio
And went to the streets to check
For what was amiss I knew not.

On the street I saw it all—
A posse of townspeople
Rushed quickly,
Panicky as hunting dogs
Racing to the scene,
Anxious,
To take a hand in capturing
The sudden news,
Now a song on the mass media.

They raced,
Haggling,
    Loud,
Pushing,
    Pulling,
Swift for a claim
To the sudden reward,

To sympathize
With the sacrifice;
The Effigy to be hanged and burnt,
Now a song on the mass media.

Clara of Lorina Club

One time glorious clap trap
Of the city,
Keep-fit of the '60s
Buxom baby, measuring the floor
Under sensual dimming lights,
A side-band at your side
At Lorina club?

Are you
The sweet sharp slim-fit
Now a sordid misfit
Of "soweto" slum
At Wandegeya?

Your soft beauty
No more a gentle glow
No more the pearliest,
Ebony eyes
Now tarnished,
You,
A tattered tartar?

Are you
Clara of Lorina club
Now time clobbered
And rifle clubbed?

Here We Are

Here we are,
Toddlers,
Left playing by ourselves,
Big brothers
Gone home to the west.

Here we are,
Budding stepbrothers;
Some veins, negroid
Others half-Hamitic.

Here we are,
Wearing weird emblems
Of black victory,
On Caucasian white flannels;
Fearing to wear each other's shoes
To learn where they pinch.

Here we are,
Racing cars of the Safari
Splashing each other
With puddle water
Going same rugged roads
To the same finish.

Predators

Predators hawk each other
To make some small ones conform
To iron-laws of gravity,
While a few big ones remain
On the high bloomy perch.

Sap bleeds into famished bround
While woodpeckers
Picking newly ripened fruits
Fly to the topmost branches
To eat more and more.

Suddenly

Sky turns dark,
Hot dusty days grow bitter in gales,
Thunder!
Grunts loud,
Visible lightning fireworkds;

At his trumpet
Thousands of fruits
And leaves fall on streets
To usher in...
The new, colder season,

We all hide in our huts
Holding our hearts.

The Freedom Embrace

For your cotton-soft hands
I loved you, my ripe banana,
Your embrace was free
Like the mother's lap.

You went incognito
And took all I had:
Your tenderness
Which was softer than butter,
Your kindness
That buttered our meals,
Your embrace,
That overshadowed my care;

You took away the grace
Which I missed
Like a heifer her dead dam's udder,
To a uniformed man
At Gaddafi barracks,
You knew I had no guts to follow.

Now peace has come to town
I search for you
Without a rude search
At the Kakira Roadblock,
I meet you on the main street,
Held sensually
By a TPDF soldier
And on Iganga Road
Embraced
By a JW soldier,
Yet on Spire Road
You are fondled
By a UNLA,
Is it you only arrested
When Jinja
Is captured to Freedom,

17

Or is it a freedom embrace
You gave me
Before the mighty
Butted,
    Booted,
Battered
    And butchered me?

The Teak Tree at Mabira

The old evergreen teak at Mabira
Towers tall and
Shakes his head in the strong foul winds.

He knows well;
Stories of a belly stuffed with bullets,
Of heads and legs, arms and parts
Of men who, after being hacked to pieces
Were dumped down mass-graves
Or on open ground buried.

Stories of a suckling child asleep,
Dead and cloven breast between its lips,
And of another child torn in two
Cutting short its last and loudest scream,
For "Ma ..." "Mama" never finished.

Old Pain

Old pain pinches new pain,
Man is money
And money is man
Who cares?

Look,
A fellow sufferer;
An ox,
Plodding Teso plains;
Stumbling,
Nodding
Like the beggar on city street
Tightly tethered on the peg of greed.

Old pain plants new pain
Power is bloodshed.

I Speared and Spilled

Well preserved,
Feigning twenty,
She fanned my soul
As the invisible wind
Does the ember.
Being thirsty at thirty
I took her the target
Worth the spear.

To my surprise,
And that of my friends
Despite counter advice
I speared a permanent blow
And the prey fell for me.
But oh,
The bad hand that aimed,
My Abraham's prayers
In vain,
Not even God's promise granted,
Ten years to date.
I speared and spilled
Worthless blood.

A Girl's Love Song

With deep leopard snarls
He bared his teeth before me;
Afraid, I was,
But he insisted, pouncing,
Licking his lips,
Eyeing me with accomplished relish.
No alternative had I
But to return a silly smile.

Like a couple of snakes,
We twisted
And turned on the path;
  He wriggled,
  Hissed
  And spat.

Leopard offered a dance
And I took part in it;
Paws wound my heart.
He hissed at the dance
And I put both legs near;
Venom swells my belly,
Hens with cocks cackle,
Scorpions raise their tails
Against me
Dashed against hard ground.

A Jilt

We fell in love too early
For quite insufficient reasons;
Tattered too late
After sufficient quiet seasons
Broken by waves of bubbling oceans.

A new light, lit for me
Is coming,
Never to go out like you,
Despite the lot you deputize.

Walk out, please,
Infatuated
By the bright dark of our day
Hounded by crazy minds
Beckoned by a hazy daylight,
Do go now before I yell.

The Love Pistol

I reach down the floor of my heart,
Feel around for the pistol of love,
Find it,
Raise it,
And fire three times at you,
Using both hands.

The first shot misses your head by an inch,
Slams into the far wall in the wilderness,
For you are too proud to love at your prime.

The second tears through your heart,
Slices half an inch of care for me
For you are too undecided to love at teenage,

The third should ricochet you off your feet
Make you fall to the floor, clutching my arm,
Your love wound, more than superficial,
Your body full of mortal care for me;
For you are adult enough to love...
Try, or else I slip the gun of love back into my heart,
Turn back the long line of haters and to my pride.

The Wedding

Her brothers and sisters
were appalled,
She brought home
such a "drag"!

Even her mother said:
"The whole house sagged,
when she and he came in!"

Her father was bewildered, too...
Trying to treat a peer
Like a son-in-law;

It was a brief ordeal for all
As the newlyweds sauntered off...
To return to their new jobs
Of wife and husband.

A Good Husband
Rarely Smokes at Home

I rarely smoke except after meals
But when Nyako rises from her seat in the bar
And her voice cracks
After a cynical smile, "*Tutaonana*" (see you, honey)
I open my briefcase with trembling fingers
And fumble to find the Embassy pack.

To soothe and smooth my feelings
I inhale slowly and steadily
One puff after another
Then grind the remains under my foot.

Ten minutes up, I dress and make up,
Before a large mirror on the Lodging Wall,
I return home, take up my position as husband
And begin wrapping up make-believe beautiful stories
To grind the remains under my foot,
For a good husband rarely smokes at home
To litter his floor with smelly ash
And bitter butts.

Njeri of Nyeri

Njeri of Nyeri scrubs her copper brown face
With Ivory soap,
And softens it with Pond's Cold Cream.
Njeri of Nyeri puts her hair up in pincurls
A clear defined part to the right
As she traverses River Road by night,
Njeri of Nyeri is fresh meat on the bait-rod;

At forty years, tender as young, musty as she is,
Njeri of Nyeri wears blue jeans or khaki pants
Or plain dark skirts,
As her four married daughters
Had done, growing up twenty-four years ago.
Njeri of Nyeri is fresh meat on the bait-rod;

Njeri of Nyeri is stern at her undefined duties
At Six Eighty Pub, Mambo Lodge and Aids Resort,
She comes off homely,
And shows her wares to black gentlemen
And white tourists on Shooting Safari,
Not ashamed to be called a *Malaya*,
Or a countrified bitch,
Njeri of Nyeri is fresh meat on the hook...
For vultures' noses
Smelling fresh meat above the sickening odour of our days.
Njeri of Nyeri's handbag is a superb magnet.

Barren Woman

You are hungry dogs in a dry land
My young brothers and sisters
Because our mother is not here,
She is in the soil
Missing our company.

She was not like this woman,
Who never feels like a parent,
Who never cares when you are hungry,
And when you are belching.

Because she is not your mother
She sends you to the market
During school time,
She does not care for your future.

Brothers and sisters,
Don't worry!
One day,
She will wash our cars,
And scrub our spacious bungalows;
If the seven of us go beyond standard seven,
Pass the 0- and A-level exams,
And train for a big office in Nairobi;
She'll cry, but no one will wipe her tears.
None of us, brothers and sisters,
Unless one of us was born to a barren mother!

No More

No More—
The day that was a fiesta,
The day we'd a sound siesta,
No more—!

No more—!
The sizzle of phonograph styluses,
The blare of Congolese jazz albums,
The dancing in the drawing room,
Many successive eves,
No more—!

No more—!
The million spectators,
Who applauded loudly,
As we sauntered, hand in hand,
Along the aisle,
No more—!

No more—
The fiesta and siesta,
And the theatre and cinema,
Where images of a wedding,
Were pinned to the foyer,
As we passed there,
No more—!

Towering over me,
You shriek at me,
With the butt ends of spite,
No longer on your knees.

Maybe a shameful lover,
Quickly looks round,
And blames the other
Not you, my stale love!

Twelve Hours

I go from office to office and back.
Discussing.
Disputing.
Motivating.
Giving up.
And beginning again
The next day.
Only to learn
Their office has refused
But
Nobody knows why.
As usual!

I move furiously
Up and down the potholed streets;
From a police station
I hear a man screaming;
They are beating him;
I wonder if he knows why!

The next day I spend twelve hours
Pushing.
Pulling.
And digging my way through life;
Their office has refused;
Everybody says *chai*!
But, nobody knows why.
As usual!

The Handicapped Handcuffed

Laden with heavy teapots
They are free to pass us—hurrying—
To buy licenses,
Pay fees or fines,
Send packages
Attend court, to win cases
Or take predetermined interview tests
They obviously pass!

Stretching languid leprous hands,
We are handicapped;
Handcuffed by strict civil procedures
Of discipline
And office hours.

We wait in long lines
With eyes glazed,
Bumping elbows,
Shifting legs——
While they go on——sipping tea.
How strict, the civil service!

Plodding clerks
Demand:
IDs, Names—tribes
Age, sex and marital status
And next of kin—
Then ten for a blank form!

From the Office Chair

I enter; he scans my clothes, bespattered with commonness.
"Sit down"... not on soft sofa, he implies
Pointing to a hard old office chair,
I sit there and stare in the air, unstared at!
"Your name?" Gruff Grumpy voice grunts,
I tell him both, "Maendeleo Uhuru."
"Strange! What tribe is your name? I'm amused!
How come you came through the gate?"
"I... I gave gatekeeper someth..."
"Some what?" He interjects grimly. I don't say more.

"I don't mean your kindness to janitor, but your business here!"
"Oh, ho! I am the farmer, whose bull won district trophy."
"What?" he seems unimpressed; impatient!
"I grow mainstays, and feed this entire city!"
"And more?" he prompts, taking notes?!
"I sent relief food to recently drought-stricken areas..."
"So what?" he derides, shattering my expectation.
"So you come to show off?" he asks.
"No sir, I would like a loan or draft... for..."
"Incredible! Loan? What for?"
"Fertilizers, spray and fees, sir!"

"Simple," he advises, "your prize winner
Will produce prize-winner milk, manure and money!
In any case, why bother about school fees?
Kids these days grow from adolescence to adultery!"
I give up hope, and am told to exit.

Pointing Fingers

The
straight
thumb
jumps
up
and
simply
laughs

The long pointer shoots ahead and blames the other for being wrong,

Three friendly fingers bent homeward
Think themselves always right.
Even the smallest, truly short.

Teeth

Is it because we're well endowed with them
That we don't hesitate showing them in pain?
Is it for the generous supply of them
That we flash them to deride and laugh?
Is it because they're long tom-tom sticks
That we flash them out in bitter songs?
Is it because they itch our lips and stink
That we jettison them to pervade the air?
Is it because they're long elephant tusks
That we display them to show their ivory worth?
Is it because they're far from the nose
That we close them at foul times, like this?
Is it because they're porcupine spines
That we snarl at each other?
Or because they're just as sharp
We don't forgive hens that cackle at us?
Or is it just because they are teeth
That we bite and bite and bite?

Rats in the Lodge

Tamed rats hunt domestic nuts
Wild rats pursue bush peas
Can't you hear:
Squeak — Squeal, screech
Over the land?

Listen,
There are rats in this lodge,
In the morning,
Squeak, squeak, like old bicycles;
During day, stark daylight,
Squeal, squeal, like pigs,
In the hot afternoon,
Screech, screech, like monkeys;
I pop up in the middle of the night, disturbed
Scream — scream, like peacocks.
What din in every room!
Squeak—Squeal—Squeeze?
Screech—Screech—Scream —
Ah—Ah—Aah!
I hate its frequency
Indiscriminate rats,
Famished.

Malaria

I soak my feet and hands in a basin of tears,
My throes and chronic malaria...
Move from joint to joint,
As the hopeless days go by, beyond the horizon.

It is worst at this joint,
It is in my pockets region,
It is in my Mathare hovel resort,
It moves from joint to joint;
One decade in the knees,
Another in the ankles.
Oh, it pains so much in the cerebellum,
I feel I rather retire...than tomorrow rise.
It roots me to one spot, head bent,
With only my mind and hands moving.

I soak my feet and hands in a pool of tears
My throes and chronic malaria
Move from joint to joint,
Rooting me to one spot, head bent,
This position stiffens the spine,
Produces exquisite aching in the calves,
Oh, it pains so much in the whole body
I feel I would rather come to the end of my shift.
Yet, the shift seems to be just half over.

City Kid

City kid can't tell goat from cat,
He calls my goatee ..."Big Cat!"
Nor cow from maid,
He calls both..."Cow!"
Mum too, scorns and scolds them so;
Nor dog from Sentry at the door,
He calls Sentry's box a kennel,
Nor dirty servant from donkey,
He carries and trudges like one!

Nor rat from rodent,
No grain granary
To kindly host them by the dozen,
As hovels and shanties in rats-nest reserves;
City kid can't contrast bare and sandaled or shoed,
He asks beggar... "Why the toes?"
He doesn't understand why some squat over pit
He says... "Pity," with spite as he spits!

City kid only knows the cat he milk-feeds
And the potbellied meat-fed puppy...
Who pounce and bounce,
Pounce and puke in the lounge or fountain;
While he too, plays indoors
With mincing miserable sister,
Peering both, at the outer-wide world
Through the small window world
Of dolls and balls,
Prams and cots
Models and dummies;
Both wincing and pissing indoors.

VIP at the Slums?

Seen a VIP visit the slums—
Camera in hand
And car-ignition key in the other?

Natives of shanty town
Take such people to be
Merely a few more tourists, come
To take a few more naked photos
For friendly postcards;
Photos of us
By them, for them,
From them to them
From year to year.

Before and After

Before and after,
Voices choke
In city streets,
In slums
Hoarse voices mumble.

Music
Booms for those in boots
Adorned with epaulettes
Commissioned,
To guard all aspects of life
In the city centre
And all suburbs yonder.

Here,
On peneplains
Truncated by silent rivers,
Here, where Earth feeds us,
Here, where clay paints huts,
voices are silent.

Only rumours about loud waterfalls
In, or near the city,
Curl on hilltops
And escape to the valley;

Here,
We only hear of messiahs in the city
Who preach the gospel
But fear the cross,
We hear rumours
Before and after the lib.

I Will Grow

Verily, verily I say unto you,
Except a grain of wheat fall
into the ground and die, it abideth
alone; but if it die, it bringeth forth much fruit.
—St. John 12:24

(Verse underlined in black in Kihika's Bible.)

The same verse vies in many heaving hearts,
In mine, it is double underlined in red
For I am betrayed to die alive
Besieged by a noose of World indifference.

I, the rootless Muyaye
Less important than Kihika, Mau Mau hero
Also hanged for the role I play,
Sharing the tongue of conspiracy
With all publicly executed;
Like Y. Y. Okot who fell
Into eternal liberation prayer
Lacerated by napalm hands
At Queen's Clock Tower
When the Muezzin at Kibuli Minaret
Prayed for peace in the land.

I, the Magendoist, a prisoner of the Economic War,
Languishing on the hard floor
In the dungeon of survival.
No air—No breath,
I, — I suffer, suffocate—
But I do not collapse;
Hope lies in unreliable endurance
No inch to turn here, alright,
But I am a liverwort spore
Now spoilt, but never split.
I will grow on this stone
South of the Sahara.

The Lady at Kisenyi

Even after the Resurrection,
Despite a teleological newday,
Untold forces, deployed
On many frontiers of her life
Besiege the lady of Kisenyi.

Only her Southern parts,
Now pulsing in ruins of war
And last night battle,
Enjoy the shadow peace
After the sweet orgasm
Brought by the blood of battle.

But,
Clouds waxing in her North
And misty waves
On the Eastern lake
Make it difficult to be sure
Whether the next day,
It will rise and shine for her,
Pearl of Africa.

The Wind and the Storm

When the wind of change rushed in,
We had just a few questions to check out.

So, we gathered around hardwood tables
To attend to vital matters of state;
But, soon fell asleep,
Under heavy munch and booze!
It was difficult to rouse us up
Even by the boom of the new anthem and gun salute
That closed suspended sessions day after day;

Subsequently,
A most violent thunderstorm
Came on…
Lasting a great part of our most productive years,
Keeping some of us constantly awake.
Many never awoke!
Despite the storm,
The buzzing new anthem and gun salute.

Sons of Wanga

A Legend of Uganda

From Moshi with foreign friends
They came,
When the Nile smelled of the people of Kintu,
Fed to fat fish and the perch,
Hacked in hecatombs,
For days that became a decade
And more...

From Kagera they marched abreast...
To sunlight the days
And moonlight the nights
Long eclipsed,

At Lukaya, they easily trounced
And triumphed, and laughed,
Sons of Wanga and friends trumpeting,
Came to Kampala and Mengo,
In one spirit,
Which, there resolutely split!

Various Frames

His car overturns in flames,
We put on various frames:
Some sob.
Others curse.

Sudden news slums our office,
We wear various invisible frames
His deputy licks lips—Posho at hand!
Others wipe him off their hands—Dirty bully boss!

The sun rises for him,
We send sad word to the ward:
Only his wife — deeply deems him dear,
Some sad—Solemnly care,
Others surprised—Call it rare!

Flocks of sigh and sympathy come
Some pay—Belated fraternity
His wife—Throws her head on stone
Others happy—Court with cups of waragi-wine,
Last funeral rites—All eat and drink to bust.

Getting Stuck

Sometime,
We stick in the same valley:
Pushing,
Pulling,
Digging,
Emptying the car,
Putting stones under the wheels:
To create friction...
Again and again...

some people had trouble
Here before us,
Things were thrown desperately around,
and in the middle...
There was an occasional grave.

Echoes to a Liberator at War

Can you hear mumbling voices
No one can understand?
I feel we are surrounded
By something we cannot see,
In the end,
I promise myself—
Never to put feet in these boots again,
So I suggest to my company,
    my country,
The whole wide world—
Never to come into it again,
If we come out alive—

Drowned in
the Murmuring Crowd

When the whisk flies
in mid-air exclamation,
my teeth become one
with those of the crowd;
when they smile their nothings,
my cheeks wrinkle.

Why do I laugh
in measurements of sweat
my lips cracking
with the stress of a slogan?

I am lost in the fidgeting crowd
stretching out my shortness
to have at least a glimpse
of the retreating convoy...

Yet I prolong my laughter
drowned in the murmuring crowd
on my journey home:

Why did I laugh
when I should have been silent
listening to the promises?

Labour Ward

Lights are off!
I can't remember
When a bulb was last here.
Anyway,
This is where we all began.
The labour ward,
Where the "weak sex" labours
To make a strong nation
And the world.
For our case,
It is the last place
Even in the numbering of wards,
The last place
For us to think about
For it'sa long since we were here.

Look,
A new arrival reminds me
Of the warm lap.
A new product of labour
Just in the dark corner beyond,
Maybe,
If immeasurable measles
Think of us,
Miserable men,
If the drugs come, soon,
That dot in a cot
Will wear a coat
Like a minister,
That small grain
Will sprout
To be what we are
But, I hope
What we aren't
For he is a *tabula rasa*.

Too Young

For Africa

Buds
On my ancestral baobab,
Big babies of the century,
Are we still young,
After decades
Of free eating from our own granary?

Why break cloudpeace
With Migs
Exchanged for our cotton?

Is it
For the sake of change
Or in search of gluttonous chance?

Maybe we will find
The dream of old age—peace
But never Canaan,
Where joy foams like juice in a gourd;
Nor any golden chance,
If we run ahead
By charging each other down.

Losing the War in Azania-Namibia

"Of late," began balding Major,
"I've noticed with dismay:
Laxity,
And loafing...
Amid your rank and file."

"Ah, ja, I see it, with distress," he said, bereaved.
"You officers never salute us seriously
Nor appear grateful for recent promotion,
What then, will the men?"

"You see people... Officers!
This kind of behavior
Among commissioned and non-commissioned;
Especially fallen infantry commanders,
This incessant dying,
This consciencelessness
This sluggishness,
Is most unfortunate for our golden cause
For the Rand;
It only points to mediocre results,
At the end of this war of decades!" he went on.

"Yes, you see, Officers and men...
We have granted you all this...
(Oval hand raises a 20 carat ring)
For this, ja, you must must march ahead,
Take cover from irresponsible dying...
Else,
I'll advise the enemy to advance on us!"
As already he is, in riots and petrol bombs.

Rascals

We heed "go back to the land" exhortations
We take development reiterations seriously,
We pay tax for *maendeleo*,
We fulfill maternal and paternal obligations
We go to coffee, tea, sisal and pyrethrum shambas
We feed and clothe, pay tithes and for essentials
We choose a simple life
Of prayer and poverty—
We support *Bulungi Bwansi* roads
We badly need *Harambee* dispensaries
And *Ujamaa* Schools and Colleges—
(To fight poverty, disease and ignorance).

Since a single figure can't kill a louse,
And many teeth together bite a bone,
We unite in *Ujamaa* brotherhood,
In a *Harambee* spirit, for peace and unity
We form *Bulungi Bwansi* Scheme (BBS)
For essential self help projects;
We donate generously with development consciousness,
Ones, tens and hundreds graduate to millions
Some thousands from the Chief, make us a fortune!
We sit and rest, assured of the best,
Progress for us at last, from our own sweat!

The rascals behind the schemes
Collect the millions behind our backs
And speedily depart
To K'La or Nbi or Dar—
To spend easily gotten gains
While we heed, "go back to the land" exhortations!

Third World War

A madman at the Kremlin
Will slay another in the Senate
Bows and arrows will be drawn
Against the slim chance left
The globe will mourn, bereft.

Elders will be taken aback,
Frenzied in panic
In a single file to the grave;
Bricks, stones and iron bars
Will be widowed, but alive,
Trees will invoke the gods,
They will slay sacrifices
Of other trees,
And smear sap libations
To cleanse the land;
But begrudged gods
Will not make amends
For they would rather have Man
Than bricks, stones and iron bars,
They will not forgive
Man for self-genocide.

Condominium
Pandemonium

A gunman storms her condominium
Shoots a girlfriend to death
Seriously wounds her brothers;
Then to justify it all (I mean his love)
Turns the weapon on himself;
Good!
So shall we in the name of love die
By none be listed as slain
Or in critical condition,
When Star Wars shall fail to shine
To restrain the nuclear pandemonium,
So shall we all fall
And uncoffined lie in our condominium.
When the button shall be pushed.

Summit on World Poverty

Renowned,
Adorned,
Dressed in brown tropical-weight suit
And white bulletproof vest
Sauntering in,
Late,
Unhurried by the lesser,
Is the host of the summit.

Deeply depressed about world poverty,
Distressed by the Poor-Rich gap;
Moved by millions of the miserable world,
Diplomats pounce the red carpet
To the north-south dialogue.
Dressed to depict the drudgery of their peoples:

High-necked formal *guyabera*,
Brilliant Kelly-green dress for ladies,
Traditional sari of the Far East,
Elegant white robes of the Levant
For the essence of the decorum,
A black three-piece and black briefcase
For many of the African entourage.

The Global Juke Box
— July 13, 1985

Fund for African Famine

We, at the Famine Relief Camp, wait,
Wriggling on empty stomachs
And rumba the night away...
Sleepless;
Nothing in hand
But saliva in wilting mouths,
Hookworms
Tapeworms
And liver flukes fluking intestines
Our potbellied kids lying or dying...

They, at the Global Juke Box
On well overfed bellies
Jazz and jive,
Twisting,
     Foxtrotting,
And break-dancing;
Males closely holding the females
Under sensual light,
Fat kids watching...
Worldwide sponsored screens
Of the extravagant extravaganza.

August First

Grey sky; and the egrets shiver in,
scribbling the cloud like white litter on the dawn.
Somewhere in the valley smoke rises, drifts
loosely through the trees.
I hear a man singing in the village
and children laugh. The voices
ruin the silence.
And my thoughts flow
in other stems, through the dried sap of my memories.
In the clear world of my past.

My memories slowly turn and watch me
like men made magic, brought to life,
who come upon me like centaurs from the hills.

If I should ride out with them in the early morning,
I would not come back.

Essay on Poetry

Poetry, rare art,
Fishes at the bottom
Of the hot dish of life,
Ladles out meat
For aesthetic pleasure
To the mouth and ear
Who dance—
While chewing.

Top layer oily soup
Often appeals
To the commonplace,
Who prefer bubbling froth
To protein.

The Eagles

Child, the eagles are flying.
Too far away for you to see
their sheaving air and pleat of flight,
splitting the feather-hook of heat with jagged cries,
wild as chaos in their claws.
Is it chance that brings them to the thermals here?
Learn from them:
they are blind earth's eyes, they
cry to the land's mask and speak to the sun.
Elements burn in them, a deep flow runs through their being.

They stack the wind and graze upon the coral heat.
Africa's birds.

Orchids

African orchids,
lion-flowers.
When the lion ghosts through the mottling grass
with the skill of the sun in his claw,
he may crush them with a paw, but the flowers have his blood.
Their sap shall cup his green edge, his subtle fire.
Though the lion walks cunning as the thorn
they shall find his moon-blood in their sipping veins.

Yet, in the half-light, they became motionless breaking waves.
I see the plunge of their whiteness,
trap of a thousand caverns in their forms.

I hear the wind on the shores of their petals.

Migrating Storks

For no apparent reason
storks have settled here
like migrating gypsies
and camp upon the village trees,
watching with deeply rooted eyes
or stretch their wings
as a fortune-teller spreads her cards.

Spreading their bays of wings
and peering thirsty-eyed around themselves
with eyes flecked like salt settled in a bowl.
They hold a silent communion
beneath the cuttle bones of clouds
or run their tongues of wings
on the wind.

To My Jogging Mate

Lead me on, keep me running through Fall,
Slowly, looking at colours,
Taking account of the value of jogging...
As for me...an exercise, adventure class!
Teach me about these trees along my new route
Taking on yellow, crimson and diverse tints
Why are those short shrubs stubbornly green?
Tell me about these temperatures chilling the trees and me
How high and low do they ever rise and fall?
Let us stop a bit, sweetheart,
Gasp, pant and rest under the coloured branches,
Feel new, soothed and thrilled by the feel of the chill.

Lead me on, keep me skating through Winter
Show me the first flakes forming on bare twigs
Like glass-rods
Tell me about icicles sticking out on the eaves
Like glass honeycombs,
I won't touch them without gloves...
For they bite and sting like the hornet.
Show me more icicles upon twigs suspended
Like stalactites in a cavern,
Sticking out on the ground
Like stalagmites rising from the floor of the cavern,
Gorgeous as golden glass mushrooms,
Show me the walls sleek and glazed
Show me all, but please don't take me out,
Frostbite is like venomous snakebite.
Keep me indoors toning and stretching,
Aerobics too, can do in the meantime;
As for water exercise, no way sweetheart, till summer.
However, on ice, sleet and snow,
Let me, every night, slide with you
Taking account of the essence of experience
For me...adventure!

Lead me on... keep me trotting through Spring
Beyond this asphalt and new tile suburbia

Into the country beyond...
Let's jog slowly looking at the paddocks,
And the pastures,
Where proud farm animals will soon graze
With sharp slurping sounds of satisfaction.
Let us stop a little bit, sweetheart
Gasp, pant and listen to the serpentine Indian Creek
As it flows with what was snow
Tell me about those spring foals and calves,
Why are they said to be large and well fed only in Spring?
Let's run on sweetheart, beyond those hills...
Let's run on into the Summer,
Take me out of the labyrinths of fur coat, gloves and hat,
As grim as the basement dungeon,
Show me the world of blossoms and blooms
Taking account of the essence of experience...
For me...adventure!
Lead me on sweetheart
Through the coloured Fall, cold Winter and Spring,
When summer comes, don't worry so much,
I'll take the lead in the jogging evenings
And tell you stories of the tropics
For it feels so much like home!
I feel I should take you home when it comes,
And show you how sweet as salt it is to sweat in summer.

A Call from Grandee

I dreamt
He called!
Hallo my *musangi*
Put this down
But never use it
Against anyone,
Keep it to heart
But never hurt anybody:

The day you came
I mean the day
You poured in
Bitter water,
Cold water
From the bottom eyes
No doubt,
I was strong
A few minutes

That day
I carried five bags
Of scarce sugar
On my back
From next shop
Across the busy road
And sold it all
In my own shop
Agile,
As I was in my prime.

She called me
To eat rice, *matoke*

And minced meat
Which I gave
A last bite,
Then a call next door
To attend
A telephone call
From someone
I was to see soon.

Putting down the receiver
It suddenly seemed
I had sent
The sound of a knell
To you all,
For the next thing
Which I never knew
Was my lying down
At dawn by my door
Never to see
Another dawn or dusk
But to hear
You,
In unison
Calling me.

She also,
Mirabu, my young wife
Too!
Didn't you see.
Her water table
Too deep to bore,
Her dry eyes turning

From side to side,
Guilty,
Unwashed
In the water
You gave me
To drink?

Remember
No frog hops into hiding
Or pops out of it
Without cause or hope;
One of you,
Truly said,
The food had not been good;
Others suspected
The telephone call
On no evidence
That my neighbour
Grudged for my shop,
Very no,
Though out of wits
I do not believe
The telephone thing.
A hawk swoops down
For his prey,
Not from afar
Does he pick it.

My *mukwano* Mirabu
Many times
Showed me signs of hate
And sometimes
For my late wife
Tolofisa's children
Whom I took to school
Since she took off
And I married Mirabu
To make
The rest of my journey
To rest down here;
So despite her ogre eyes
I returned an ogle
To requite her kindness
In cooking the stuff

Such as I ate
Just before I went off
Without a will.

People say
It's the kite
Who picks chicks
But they forget
A depraved dog
Or even a hen
In their midst
Who pecks eggs.

Remember
When elders convened
To take an impartial
But calculated look
Into my material records;
When my dear wife,
Mirabu
Said without any fear
I owed her
Twenty shillings
For my life
And asked the treasurer
Of your belated alms
Not to forget her
At the sharing
Of responsibilities.

You saw her
Given her treasure,
So and so, the cows
Some, the houses
Others this,
And that—
Gosh!
My children,
My blood,
My *musangi*,
My all,
For whom I sweated
To death for a lifetime
Nothing!

That doesn't matter
Anymore
For me
And many souls here
Provided Bukya
Who took my shoes
Takes my children to school
And for safety,
Baliddawa
Drives the remains of my home
At a good speed,
Taking Namugabo
On board
With insight
That her son,
My *musangi*
Will be the poet
To receive this
Secret message
And sing
To the world
Many other songs.

I would not ring
To you my *musangi*
Because here
There is no mint
And a reverse call
Is too expensive
For young people
Like you,
Only old people
Like my heir
Must afford it
But even then
I must call

Before he comes
For he should care
For Tigasitwa
And tell Baliruno
Life is never in the bottle
Which is too narrow

And the beer too bitter
To swallow.

Remember
For me
And the village vicar
Thought for a gourd
Was too shallow;
That is why
You came to sing for me
In state
With bibles in hand,
As a host of white collars
Requiemed.

This is why
I would leave Mirabu alone
Meandering with all sizes of men
Until one day, she also
Will close her eyes
Praying to me to accept her back
For in here, it is always so.

Already, good Lord,
I have rejoined Tolofisa
Though she cooks not
For we do not need it,
I am cocksure
Mirabu also
Will be happy one day
To rejoice here with us
For when we parted
I was innocent,
Though before the grim law
Of the Elders
I owed her twenty shillings
For which
She sent me into this mine
To find a job
Over and out.

Childhood Memories

For Grammy

So she used to say,
With her chin cupped in her hand,
Her knife in her armpit,
"You'll sit in the banana plantain
Wishing to see me;
Wishing to talk to me,"
And I took it for a fireside joke.

So she used to mutter,
Her pipe posed in her mouth
With her knife picking cinders to smoke,
"You'll call but I'll not answer,
You'll ask but there'll be no answer,"
And I took it for a stereotyped stammer.

So she used to foretell,
So she used to foresee,
Her evil finger on the ground
Counting remaining time;
"I'll drop my knife into this soft ground
Wishing to see it again
Wishing to see it again."
And I took it very lightly.

Now I see what she used to say,
I call, but there is no answer,
Elders have kept her underground
In a musty brown bark cloth.

The Black Pot of Potatoes

In the festive mood of Uhuru
Hurrying to be free,
We tore wood out of a dry hedge
Perfunctorily put it between wooden supports,
Our black pot of potatoes on top.

Soon,
A fire roared under the pot
Making nearby trees sweat,
Opposite banks quiver
Swimming in heat.

As soon,
Flames
Burnt through the wooden supports;
Upside down with a thud
Hissed the pot into the midst of flames.

The original pot-lid so flown off,
Rushing water,
And the young flying potatoes
Tickled a heavy cloud of steam from the fire,
Which scalded many a soul
Who tried to rescue the pot.

At long last the pearly black pot
Was settled by gallant neighbours
Who for us put it upright on the embers.

Among us, many male cooks,
Too hungry to wait for wives' dishes
Poured in more water
And added armfuls of dry wood.

Salivating women and children
Spread palm-leaf mats under shady trees
Waiting to feast—
Alas, the pearly black pot tumbled again
Tickling more steam from the fire.

Smithies in Kisenyi

Day and night
Smithies in Kisenyi
Never close,
Drunken blacksmiths there
Never tire, like fire in dry brush.

Mallets,
Held by both hands
Hit anvils.

The mallet
Nods up and down
Eager to explore
All sides and corners
Of the anvil.

The anvil sweats
In the experience,
    Sweet,
    Burdensome,
    Cumbersome,
She sweats on,
Now slippery
And squelching
In sweat,
And mallet lubricant
Sobs and shouts.

Nearby blacksmiths
Who overhear,
And anvils
Who eavesdrop,
Also erect and imitate,
Then you hear mixed echoes;
The ground squeaking,
Mallets groaning,
Anvils screeching,
Away to the corners of K'la
Blind to time and place.

As I pass by, I spit;
For the burning smell
Of musty metal nauseates me,
I see a staggering blacksmith
Tired, withdrawing his mallet,
Going out to repose.
I hear the anvil sighing
Maybe to rest,
Waiting for another onslaught.

I pity the metal industry in the nation,
For the metal they hit in Kisenyi smithies
May not be the future mallet
Nor the anvil,
It is too rusty!

Greetings

The Chagga greet you with a smile
"*Keti Kidenguni!*" they cry, handing you a chair,
With warm handshake,
Mum greets "*Shamsha mani?*"
If you're a fellow mum
Or "Shamsha lai ?"
If you're a dad,
Handing you a *kata*—*calabush* of *pombe*
"*Nakwaft mani!*" you should say
To thank mum for brewing and bringing banana beer
One equal greets "*Shamsha ndraa?*"
The other replied "*Shamsha yee!*"
The general reply like "I'm alright!" very conventional;

The handshake is important in Kisii
You don't just say "*Bwakire?*" in the morning
Marching past your villagemate or a stranger,
As if you have diarrhea!
Or "*Bwailire?*" in the afternoon and eve,
Plodding on, like the coming night
Is a charging lion, coming towards you!
You must stop, clap hands together,
Shake them up and down for long...

Raise each other's hand to your face or lick it,
To show *amasikani*, respect, honour!
Only a Pharisee or self-centered stranger
Would withdraw or withhold his hand
Or even one carrying feces on hand!
Even two people who have quarrelled
Never hide hands in greeting...
Gusiis also say "*Ikara nsa!*" offering you a chair.

Soga and Ganda have fewer handshakes,
Only intimates for intimacy's sake, shake hands:
A lady at a tryst with her *younkee wight*
Parents and child returning home after long...
Or close friends for close affection's sake
And respect,
Never so with strangers a lot, especially on the street.
And most cases at home, not as much as the Gusii
Probably, for the same reasons whites wouldn't kiss.

The female kneels down for whom she respects and reveres
Though women's liberation has taken her halfway off her knees
For these days, she half kneels, half stands!
The male stands akimbo at attention
Like we do at national flag raising...then greets,
Looking straight into the other's face
Not bending to hide his eyes like the thief
Or the promiscuous.
Who fears recognition and contempt.
Before in-laws the Soga male must sit on a chair
With his legs closed together,
So that mother-in-law doesn't imagine a thing
Between them!
When he is escorted to the road, he squats down
To say goodbye.

Most African greetings ask for one's health
And that of the people living far off
Where one rains from.
And whether it rises and shines,
Or winds and rains,
Or hails for the people there.

Todate, someone knocks at our door,

We panic
Peep and peer through the window
Halfway open the door:
"Good evening!" We coldly say.
"What can I do for you?"
He has nothing special!
Nothing for us to get; or take seriously,
We leave him by the door staring...
If he's a stranger we suspect
We send Pillar to bark him away...
If he does fear dogs, he goes, if not...
We pass him by the door steal, staring...
"See you later!" We say to him, still waiting.

Nobody says "*Umuofia kwenu!*" like the Ibo,
Before Parliament sits
Greetings are not in the immunities and privileges code,
Nobody greets before the court sits,
Nobody says "*Uzeulu*, I greet your body."
The law books don't spell out that statute!
If a madman said "*Umuofia kwenu!*"
No one in his senses would reply "*Yaa!*"!?
For these are modern years, hallelujah,
We pass a pal on the way,
And wave coldly like monkeys
Or, "How're you!" We quickly quip...
Then away in a hurry down the road,
As if he caused our burden and load:
Business houses, busy offices and business hours!

A Paean for P'Bitek

Every time I met him
I learnt something rich
Something the man himself;

At the Pillars of Nuisance
Towering at Makerere hill
I met him,
Talking softly to a friend
Going to his home of Arts.
Eagerly I pulled up to them
And called him "Sir"
Stretching my hand
Which he didn't take.

As a dog scans a shilling
He looked at me,
Calmly laid hand on my head
Sadly touched, deeply moved.

Never address an African as "Sir"
He counselled,
Only knighted Britishers are.
"I am Okot P'Bitek" he said
And walked away
Leaving me.

That was years ago.
Now,
He has bowed out of the race,
He has left me wiping face
Just trotting,
A tired dog, gasping for breath
Weeping in the wilderness
For his shots missed,
    Undetonated,
Blown wide and wild
    By the foul wind.

Oh, his tongue shot at Tina
    And Ocol the buffoon,
His pen fired the *malaya*
    And pinched her dirty bottoms,
His shots that missed

71

Were heard far and wide
All over the world,
He was a webbed duck
Who stood on the fierce Nile
Perched on flaming sand
By the banks of the river
And many times flew away
Over the turbulence of Owen Falls Dam.

He quacked for help
In the dark days of his day
He quacked songs and songs—;
Song of Lawino
Song of Ocol
Song of Malaya
Song of Prisoner,
Songs of small fish
Stifled by Nile perch.

He quacked long and loud
Till one day,
The stile broke away
Leaving wounded me sad.
Singing a dirge
For the rejected cornerstone
Who rejected padres
Who parrot the gospel
But eat the fruits underground.
A Franz Fanonian voice
Live in the Sahara
Spreading South in our times,
A red hot iron of irony
Burrowing loopholes of our day

Lost,
The East African style,
Venomous,
Sharp
As the sting of a wasp.

I weep the wick
Of a lamp,

Extinguished

I see the fire
On Makerere hill
Fierce
Now extinguished,
Spear-tip
Now blunted.

Gone up
The kite-beak
Who pecked without nausea
The dunghills of his day.

GLOSSARY

Kilembe Mines: Copper mines in the Kasese District of Western Uganda.

At the Celebration of Freedom: *Freedom Square.* Open air parks set apart for celebrating national holidays, like Independence, Republic, or Liberation day.

Termites: *Magendoist.* See "I Will Grow."

25TH of January: *January 25, 1971.* The day Idi Amin carried out the coup d'etat that ousted Milton Obote.

Clara of Lorina Club: *Lorina.* A night club popular in the 1960's. Soweto. Slum area near Makerere University, named by University students after the South African Black Township. Students used to go there to drink beer which they called "rioting." *Wandeyeya.* A shopping area near Makerere University, part of which is the slum called "Soweto."

The Freedom Embrace: *Gaddafi.* Army barracks in Jinja, Uganda, named after Muamer Gaddafi of Libya by Idi Amin, his ally. Before the 1971 coup, these barracks were known as the the Uganda Army First Battalion. *Kakira Road Block.* Throughout Amin's regime, his army kept strict road blocks on all the major roads in the country, especially at the entry points of cities and towns. *Kakira.* Suburb of Jinja town where such a road block was mounted. *UNLA (Uganda National Liberation Army).* The rebel army that fought Idi Amin—Collaborating-in-arms with UNLA were TPDF (Tanzanian People's Defense Forces) and J.W. (Jeshi La Wakombozi: Liberation Army of Tanzania. *Jinja.* Industrial town of Uganda.

The Teak Tree at Mabira: *Mabira.* A tropical rain forest halfway between Jinja and Kampala, characterized by tall teak, elm and mahogany trees entwined with creepers. In it were dumped lynched men and women, victims of dictatorships.

Old Pain: *Teso Plains.* Flat grassland in Eastern Uganda where most traditional farmers use oxen to plough. *Nyeri.* A district in Central Kenya. *Malaya.* Whore, prostitute, or any promiscuous woman.

Barren Woman: *Nairobi.* A fast growing and attractive city in Kenya, headquarters of the United Nations Environmental Agency, HABITAT; also the capital of Kenya, having tourist attractions and commercial facilities. Many young people in East Africa look forward to the day when they will finish college and go to work and live in this city. It contrasts sharply with the impoverished villages and shanties.

Twelve Hours: *Chai*. Kiswahili, meaning tea. An euphemism for bribe, tip or baksheesh.

Malaria: *Mathare*. A mushrooming rundown shanty village in Nairobi City, Kenya, contrasting sharply with the city's skyscrapers. The "malaria" that people of Mathare suffer from is physical, mental, economic and political, not always carried by mosquitoes.

Before and After: *The Lib*. Short for the Liberation from Amin's dictatorship.

I Will Grow: *Kihika*. A character, betrayed by his fellow natives, to the British Officials during the War for Independence, popularly called the Mau Mau War, in Kenya. Kihika is in Ngugi Wa Thiong's novel, *A Grain of Wheat*. *Muyaye*. A slang word developed in Uganda in the 1970's as a nickname for black marketeers, bums, and teenagers who took to the streets of Ugandan towns to sell hoarded commodities. *Y.Y. Okot*. The Chief Education Officer of Uganda during Amin's time. He was suspected of dissidence, arrested and killed by a firing squad at Queen's Clock Tower in Kampala. *Kibuli*. One of the seven hills of Kampala, site of the biggest Mosque in Uganda. *Magendoist*. Comes from magendo, Swahili word meaning "black market," "hot' trade," "corrupt transaction." A magendoist practices *magendo*. Sometimes he overdresses to impress people. He is a dude—can also be a woman.

The Lady of Kisenyi: *Lady of Kisenyi*. Refers to a whore of the Kampala slums, a personification of Uganda during the Liberation War.

Sons of Wanga: *Moshi*. Town in Northern Tanzania, East Africa, where Ugandan rebels convened the Uganda National Liberation Front (UNLF) in 1979, which in collaboration with Tanzanian troops overthrew Idi Amin by marching on Kampala, capital of Uganda on 11 April. *Kintu*. Patriarch of the Baganda, largest tribe in Uganda. A religious cult invokes the spirit of Kintu, when trouble comes. *Kagera River*. Boundary between Southern Uganda and North West Tanzania. Amin's troops held up Ugandan rebels and Tanzanian troops for several days. The liberators had to repair the bridge before they followed Amin's troops inside Uganda. *Lukaya*. A small town south of Kampala. The Tanzanian troops and Ugandan rebels fought another decisive battle here against Amin's troops.

Mengo. One of seven hills that compose Kampala, site of the palace of the Kabaka (King) of Buganda, whom the first Prime Minister of independent Uganda, Milton Obote, deposed and drove into exile in Britain, where he died. When Idi Amin came to power he brought the Kabaka's remains back to Uganda and held a state funeral.

Various Frames: *Posho.* A kind of porridge made by mingling corn meal in hot water until it is hard, then served with gravy or greens. In the poem it is like "bread and butter," the stuff of life and prosperity. *Waragi* (Uganda) or *Changaa* (Kenya and Tanzania). A drink with high alcoholic content that people in East Africa illicitly brew. Uganda has a distillery where the impure stuff is purified into legal Uganda Waragi. However, most people drink the illicit brew because it is cheaper and stronger.

Drowned in the Murmuring Crowd: *Whisk.* The cow's tail switch is dried to make a prestigious device to whisk flies off a dignitary who carries it as people carry umbrellas. African politicians sometimes use it to gesticulate at political rallies.

Losing the War in Azania-Namibia: *Azania.* The original name of the Republic of South Africa. *Namibia.* The African name of Southwest Africa, illegally ruled by the racist regime in South Africa. The country is named after the Namib Desert. Both the ANC (African National Congress) and SWAPO (Southwest African People's Organization) are fighting the racist regime for independence. The poem looks at the war from the eyes of a racist general. *The Rand.* Short for Witwatersrand, a mineral rich region upon which the city of Johannesburg in South Africa has sprouted. This region is known for its gold and other mineral wealth.

Rascals: *Maendeleo.* (Kiswahili) Development, especially of the nation's economics. *Bulungi Wansi.* Literally means "for the good of the nation," a name for voluntary collective projects for civil development in Uganda, a Lugunda expression. *Horambee.* (Kiswahili) A popular political chant in Kenya, meaning "Let us work together for development," the avowed spirit of Kenya. *Ujamaa.* This means "brotherhood" in Kiswahili, the spirit of Tanzania, which calls for collectivity and socialism for development. *K'la.* Short for Kampala City (Uganda). *N'bi.* Short for Nairobi city (Kenya). *Dar.* Short for Dar-es-Salaam City (Tanzania).

Summit on World Poverty: *Guyabera.* A very elegant dress.

August First: *August 1, 1982.* Date of attempted coup d'etat in

Nairobi, Kenya. The city was looted clean, but the coup was countered in a few hours by loyal sovereign troops. This event conjured up memories of what had happened in Uganda on 25th January 1971.

A Call from Grandee: *Grandee*. Grandfather. *Musangi*. Means "fellow husband." Among the Basoga of Uganda, it is believed that a son is a reincarnation of his grandfather. Therefore, grandfathers refer to grandsons as "musangi." Granddaughters are reincarnations of their own grandmothers. Their grandfathers call them "wife." *Matooke*. A delicious meal of mashed bananas served with gravy or peanut stew, cherished by the people of Southern Uganda, a staple before it became prohibitively expensive during the 1970's. *Mukwano Mirabu*. Means "Darling Mirabu." Mirabu or Mebra is a woman's Christian name. My grandfather's third and last wife was Merabu. They had a bad domestic misunderstanding over my late grandmother's children, because Merabu hated them. When my grandfather died, it was suspected that Merabu had something to do with the death—that she cast the spell that caused it. *Tigasitwa*. Second maternal uncle. *Bukya*. My grand-uncle, heir to my grandfather. *Baliddawa*. My first maternal uncle. *Namugabo*. My mother's name. *Baliruno*. My third maternal uncle who fell out of school because Mirabu would not let my grandfather pay the fees. *Torofisa*. My grandmother, who died before my grandfather remarried Mirabu.

The Black Pot of Potatoes: *Uhuru*. Kiswahili word meaning "independence" or "freedom."

Smithies in Kisenyi: *K'la*. Abbreviation for Kampala.

Greetings: *Chagga*. A Bantu tribe dwelling mainly in the Rombo District of Tanzania, at the foothills of Mt. Kilimanjaro. *Shamsha Mani* (*Chagga*). "How are you, madam?" "Madam" means a respectable senior lady. *Shamsha Lai* (*Chagga*). "How are you, Sir?" *Kata* (*Chagga*). A calabash used for serving beer, home-brewed from bananas, the first thing a guest is treated to before the host or hostess extends a handshake in greetings. *Nakwafo Mani* (*Chagga*) "Thank you mum or madam." *Shamsha Hdraa* (*Chagga*). "How are you, my friend," or "Hi, Pal ! *Shamsha Yee* (*Chagga*). "I'm fine, my friend/ I'm all right, thanks." *Kisii*. A Bantu tribe living in the Kisii Hills of Kenya. The people are called Abagusii, their language, Ekegusii, their district, Kisii. *Bwakire* (*Ekegusii*). "Good morning?" *Bwairire* (*Ekegusii*). "Good afternoon ?" *Amasikani* (*Ekegusii*). Respect, honor or civility. *Ikara Nsa* (*Ekegusii*). Take a seat, or sit down. *Ganda* or *Baganda*. Another

Bantu tribe living in the Southern Heartland of Uganda, who actually gave the country its name. Their language is called Luganda. **Soga** or **Basoga**. Another Bantu tribe living on the northern shores of Lake Victoria, in Uganda. Their language is called Lusoga. **Pillar**. A dog's name. **Ibo**. A tribe that mainly inhabits the Eastern Province of Nigeria, West Africa. **Umuofia Kwenu (Ibo)**. Used in greetings at meetings, like: "How are you, Kansas City?" Adapted from Chinna Achebe's book, *Things Fall Apart*. **Uzeulu (Ibo)**. Male name. **Yaa**. A loud cry meaning, "Yes !" An affirmation, especially at a rally or civil meeting.

A Paean for P'Bitek: *Okot P'Bitek* (1931-1982). Ugandan poet and social anthropologist, whose work had an enormous influence throughout Africa: *Song of Lawino* (1966), *Song of Ocol* (1970), and *Two Songs* (1971). **Pillars of Nuisance**. Huge cement pillars that stand in front of the Arts Complex at Makerere University, Kampala, Uganda. **Tina**. Tina is the African version of Clementine, a character in Okot P'Bitek's *Song of Lawino*, who represents a lost westernized African woman who no longer practices African folkways and clashes with the ideals of the indigenous "ideal woman." **Ocol**. Also a character in Okot P'Bitek's *Song of Lawino*, representing the "educated," westernized African who neither fits African ways nor Western ways; a half-baked cultural caricature. **Lawino**. The main character in *Song of Lawino*, a traditional girl still stuck to the old ways of the tribe, who conflicts with Tina and Ocol because of culture-lag and estrangement in Africa. **Frantz Fanon**. Born in Martinique and educated in France, a psychiatrist who wrote about the psychology of suffering subjects of colonialism (*The Wretched of the Earth*). Okot P'Bitek has a poem entitled "Song of Malaya" (from *Fired the Malaya*). *Malaya* means "prostitute."

Alfred T. Kisubi is now distinguished professor of human services, multicultural and global education at the University of Wisconsin-Oshkosh, where he teaches courses in drug abuse, domestic violence and task groups in human services. He completed his undergraduate studies in literature, sociology and political science at Makerere University in Uganda. He then taught high school English language courses in literature, English as a second language, and religious education for eleven years in Uganda and four years in Kenya. In Uganda he carried out research in water usage habits in Uganda towns for the World Bank feasibility study for rehabilitation, and also in puerperal psychosis. He was also a national examiner of literature exams for the Kenya National Examination Council.

In 1985, Kisubi came to the United States as an exchange consultant in African studies and instructor of sociology at Johnson County Community College in Overland Park, Kansas. He completed an MA in sociology and PhD in administration of higher education at the University of Missouri-Kansas City. His doctoral research investigated race relations and their implications for the administration of higher education on a Midwestern campus.

Kisubi is also the author of *Race and Ethnicity in the First Person* (with Michael Burayidi, Greenwood Press) and a contributor to numerous books on human services and multiculturalism. His other poetry collections include *Kalulu the Hare in Exile, Maybe It's a Dream, Storms: Poems of Azania*, and *Hi*. He founded and runs a study abroad seminar about Africa's experience of globalization and development. As a humanist poet and human services worker he sits on the Advisory Board of African Americans for Humanism and that of the Oshkosh Salvation Army. He is on the Editorial Board of *Free Inquiry*, a journal of the International Council of Secular Humanism.

CPSIA information can be obtained at www.ICGtesting.com
Printed in the USA
LVOW122253161211

259855LV00001B/4/A